LETTERS FROM
Stella

BETTY WOOD OGLESBEE

CONTENTS

ACKNOWLEDGEMENTS

Without the helpful assistance of Dr. Richard Van Praagh, _Letters from Stella_ would not have been possible. I sincerely appreciate the detailed information and photographs provided by Dr. Van Praagh in regard to Stella's personal and professional life.

I am indebted to my husband John Oglesbee, whose paper entitled _"East Texas Metamorphosis during World War II"_ formed a significant part of Chapter One. His paper was presented at a conference titled _"No Ordinary Time: East Texas in World War II: The Home Front"_ hosted by the Department of History, Stephen F. Austin State University, Nacogdoches, Texas, on April 8, 1995.

Thanks so much to friends Laquita Ledford Elliott and Gwendolyn Hall Odom, as we remembered together and clarified the details of our days as Girl Scouts in 1945-46.

Thanks as well to my cousin Hazel Faye Sanders Andre, for her recollections of corresponding with Stella's friend Cybele during the late 1940s.

INTRODUCTION

San Augustine, Texas
1945

*A*nna Fay sat beside the radio and cried tears of relieved emotion. It was May 7, 1945. The newscaster had announced, "Germany has surrendered unconditionally. Victory in Europe is assured."

I remember asking, already knowing the answer, "Mother, are you all right?" Until that moment, we hadn't been sure that America and the Allied forces would win against the forces of evil perpetrated by the Axis powers. Then, during the early months of 1945, the tide had begun to turn in our favor. We listened to radio reports, read newspaper accounts of the war's progress, and rushed to "The Augus Theatre," our downtown movie house, to watch the short "News of the Day" clips picturing weekly happenings of the conflict. There was a renewed and growing hope for success.

"Of course I am, Betty. Our boys will be coming home, and perhaps we can put these dark days of war behind us.

But we grieve for the ones whose lives were lost for freedom's sake, and for the people of Europe and elsewhere in the world whose homelands are destroyed."

By August 14, 1945, Japan, too, had agreed to terms of surrender. August 15, 1945 was declared V-J Day. The fighting was truly over.

I could not begin to imagine that less than a year later, in 1946, I would become friends with a young girl from across the world, in Crete, Greece, and the "Letters from Stella" would begin.

CHAPTER ONE

*San Augustine and the Rural
East Texas Transformation:
1941 and the Early War Years*

*S*an Augustine is the Eastern Gateway to Texas. Situated directly on *El Camino Real de los Tejas National Historic Trail*, it has been the route of choice for travelers entering or leaving Texas, beginning in 1691. World War II was no exception. This road, State Highway 21, became the thoroughfare for troop movements across Texas to Fort Polk in Louisiana. It was a familiar sight in San Augustine to see army vehicles filled with soldiers headed in an easterly direction toward their destination. Winning the war was crucial to the survival of our country, and we all knew it.

Radio announcers and newspapers with bold headlines reported the bombing of Pearl Harbor by the Japanese Air Force on December 7, 1941, a clandestine deed followed on December 11 with Germany and Italy declaring war on the United States. These events were to initiate a riptide of change throughout America, and certainly in the small town of San Augustine, creating an irrepressible movement that was to forever modify the traditions of the people in a peace-loving land. In rural East Texas, the easygoing lifestyles of the inhabitants were quickly and relentlessly eroded away. No longer could the dense pine forest shield our people from the happenings of the outside world, and vestiges of change began appearing on every hand.

Defense-oriented slogans appeared on signs in public places everywhere, in courthouses, post offices, and rail-road depots. On large red, white, and blue posters, Uncle Sam pointed his finger at all passersby with the urgent message: "I Want You for the U.S. Army...Enlist Now!" Office of War Information (OWI) photographer John Vachon came to San Augustine in 1943, capturing many of these images for posterity. The young men of San Augustine and the Deep East Texas area responded overwhelmingly to the call. Many joined the various branches of military service, Army, Navy, Air Force, and Marines, while others came through the Selective Service System. An innate spirit of patriotism swelled within the breasts of Americans both young and old.

Like many rural communities, a "home guard" composed of predominately older men not enlisted in military service was formed in San Augustine for protection against possible enemy attack. The "San Augustine County Council of Defense" was well organized, meeting regularly for drills and practice with firearms.

As the mass exodus of men into the military continued, countless thousands of jobs in shipyards, defense facilities, and various other commercial enterprises were created. Many of the remaining men in San Augustine County left their farms to work in the shipyards on the Gulf Coast. These openings in some cases were filled by women as well, as they abandoned the traditional roles within their homes and communities.

In San Augustine, women of the town gathered in large numbers in the second-floor dance hall of the 1883 Hollis Building to wrap bandages for the war effort. Everyone became aware of the concept and necessity of conserving. The saying came into vogue, "Use it up, wear it out, make it do, or do without." People planted Victory Gardens behind their homes, purchased war bonds, and paid strict attention to food and gasoline rationing. Many dashboards of local cars had a small sign with the words, "Is this trip really necessary?" School children did their part by buying small amounts of defense stamps during home room periods.

Camp San Augustine, a branch of Camp Fannin in Tyler, Texas, housed German POWs, mostly from Rommel's Afrika Corps. The men had been brought to San Augustine in early 1944. They worked in the East Texas forests, harvesting large amounts of timber damaged in recent ice storms, and were paid 80 cents per day. The POW camp was located on the old San Augustine County fairgrounds, securely fenced, well-lit, with round-the-clock guards. "Camp San Augustine was not a tough place to be a POW. The young men, mostly in their early twenties, were given a good ration, and allowed to play soccer, a favorite sport in Europe long before the game became popular in the United States."[1]

The Keidel family lived across the street from the POW camp. They were of German descent, and owned a bakery in downtown San Augustine. Each day Mrs. Keidel would bring her leftover baked goods for the prisoners. She would play the piano for them each evening, the music of their homeland wafting from her opened windows into the ears of the prisoners across the street. After the war, her daughter Amelia

Keidel married one of the prisoners, Otto Rinkenauer, who had been a boxing champion in Germany.

Camp San Augustine closed in April 1946, remaining in operation longer than any other East Texas POW branch facility.

The World War II conflict created a lasting legacy of change throughout all of America, and certainly in Texas, expanding the horizons of our people and providing opportunities beyond imagination. "Along the Gulf Coast the greatest petrochemical industry in the world was built to refine fuel for the American war machine. Farmers cultivated soil to its maximum, helping the United States become the granary for the Allied nations. Wartime industries mushroomed throughout Texas: steel mills, enormous aircraft factories, extensive shipyards, a revitalized paper and wood pulp industry, and munitions factories. The largest tin smelter in the world was built at Texas City."[2] At the war's end in 1945, our country had emerged physically unscathed, but the priceless treasure of the young men whose lives were given in defending our way of life cannot, even to this day, be measured adequately.

Somehow, we continue to strive toward achieving the elusive goals of international harmony and peace. Are we trying hard enough? Are we doing our best? These are hard questions that beg for answers.

Young Medical Doctor Stella Zacharioudakis visited my family in San Augustine at Christmastime, 1955. Most of the locales mentioned in Chapter One remained intact after the span of ten years since the war's end. We drove everywhere around the region during Stella's five-day stay with us, giving her the Grand Tour of the various points of interest in our area: the historic homes, many dating back to Republic of Texas days; the Hollis building, where the women of San Augustine wrapped bandages for the war effort; the native-stone high school gym, where the members of the San Augustine County Council of Defense met regularly; the site of the POW Camp in San Augustine; and the red brick Keidel home across the street. She attended church with us. We traveled down the historic *El Camino Real*, remarking on the many footsteps that had trod that ancient roadway into Texas. She laughingly questioned our "ancient" terminology. In Greek thinking, *El Camino Real* would be considered a new road.

In her remarkably brilliant and thoughtful way, Stella responded to our East Texas hospitality with grace and enjoyment. During those few short days, I realized that her ability to identify with others was one of her great strengths. I have never known a person with a more caring spirit than my friend Stella. Her visit with my family is a treasured memory, never to be forgotten.

CHAPTER TWO

Greece in World War II
and
Stella's Home, Rethymnon, Crete

*E*ach year Greece celebrates the anniversary of "OXI" Day, a significant event which occurred on October 28, 1940. On that day, "the Greeks rejected an ultimatum from the dictator Benito Mussolini to allow Italian troops on Greek soil or else. The Greeks responded with the now historic word 'OXI' which means 'NO' in Greek. When attacked by Axis forces, the Greeks stood their ground, and would not accept defeat. News of Greece's victory flooded the airwaves and covered the front pages of newspapers around the globe. A grateful world celebrated as against all odds (that) such a small nation derailed the seemingly unstoppable Axis forces. The historical significance of this day and what it meant to the outcome of World War II cannot be overstated. It was one of the most consequential victories for freedom and democracy in the modern world."[3]

"If there had not been the virtue and courage of the Greeks, we do not know which the outcome of World War II would have been."
Winston Churchill

"(We) thank the Greek people, whose resistance decided WW II.... You fought unarmed and won, small against big....You gave us time to defend ourselves."
Joseph Stalin

"When the entire world had lost all hope, the Greek people dared to question the invincibility of the German monster, raising against it the proud spirit of freedom."
Franklin Delano Roosevelt

"Greece resisted the Axis powers for over 185 days, from October 28, 1940 to April 31, 1941."[3] Having secured the mainland, Hitler's forces planned an airborne attack on the airfields of Crete, namely, Maleme, Rethymnon, and Heraklion. During the invasion of May 20, 1941 "The German paratroopers met fierce resistance upon landing. Stunned by the high losses his troops sustained, Hitler resolved never to conduct a major airborne attack again."[4] Ten days were required before the Germans were able to occupy Crete.

"Hence, we will not say that Greeks fight like heroes, but that heroes fight like Greeks."
Winston Churchill

MAP OF CRETE, SHOWING THREE LOCATIONS OF AIR ATTACKS.

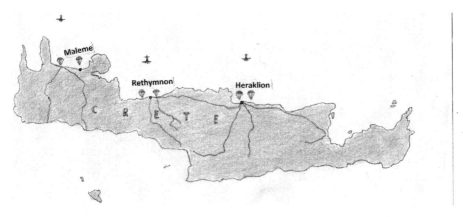

...DRAWING BY SARA OGLESBEE

"The Greek Resistance played a large role during the years 1942, 1943 and 1944. Mainland Greece was liberated in October 1944 with the German withdrawal in the face of the advancing Red Army."[5]   Only after the war's end were Crete and the Aegean Islands free of the German presence. "The country was devastated by war and occupation, and its economy and infrastructure lay in ruins."[5]

The island of Crete, Greece in the 1940s was Stella Zacharioudakis' homeland, a locale subjected to harsh, hurtful, life-changing events. She was there, through it all. Stella and her family, consisting of her parents Constantine and Eleni (Helen in English), and her siblings Mary, Lefteris (Elefterios in Greek, meaning Freedom), Victoria, and Yiannis (John in English) survived the German airborne attack, and persevered during the subsequent occupation of Crete.

The "unquenchable spirit" exhibited by the Greek people during those perilous days was a significant part of her heritage. As a twelve year old girl reading the "Letters from Stella" written to me, only on one occasion, when she mentioned the death of her father, did I detect sadness and loss. She was forever positive, focused on the good things in life, the beauty of nature, learning, and achieving her goal of becoming a medical doctor. Stella was an amazing young woman who did not allow circumstances beyond her control to dominate her life, but strove with that Greek-inspired "unquenchable spirit" to do her best.

CHAPTER THREE

Girl Scouts with a Purpose

During the years 1945 and 1946 my eleven and twelve year old friends and classmates looked forward to our weekly Girl Scout meetings. We especially liked our leaders, Mrs. Georgia Mathews and Mrs. Sarah Grambling, who were two of our favorite teachers in the San Augustine schools. Girls in our troop were *Laquita, Paula, Evva Dene, Gwendolyn, Jane Teel, Martha, Rosemary, Jean, Jeanette, Pat, Frances, Sarah, and me. We proudly wore our uniforms while participating in service projects in our local area. Hiking and camping were enjoyable activities, although building a fire rubbing two sticks together was less than successful.

In an early January meeting in 1946, the girls in our troop were presented the idea for an activity that would extend our local outreach. Miss Georgia offered us the opportunity to send small, handmade gift bags overseas as a thoughtful reminder to girls in war torn countries that we truly cared about them. With the end of the war still so fresh on our minds, we immediately said, in unison, "Yes, let's do this!" This would be a memorable and rewarding experience, a means through which we could help in some small way.

As I reminisced about this long-ago project, I decided to contact the New York headquarters of Girl Scouts of the USA concerning the logistics of how this particular program was developed. I spoke with Senior Archivist Yevgeniya Gribov, in the National Historic Preservation Center, Girls Scouts of the USA, who was extremely helpful with her answers. I quote from her email reply to my inquiry:

"In Girl Scouts national archives we have an extensive set of files on the World War II defense effort. I can confirm that Girl Scouts of the USA demonstrated strong dedication to service to their country during World War II. After the bombing of Pearl Harbor, Girl Scouts headquarters sent a telegram to all councils saying 'Girl Scouting IS defense' and urged Girl Scouts to 'stick to their jobs.' Throughout the war, Girl Scouts participated in numerous service projects, including collection of necessities to be shipped to Europe."

Hours were spent during our local Girl Scout meetings in planning and implementing our project. Each of our bags was hand-sewn of substantial twill fabric with a drawstring closure, and filled with soap, washcloth, toothpaste, toothbrush, and safety pins. A short letter written by each girl was placed inside her bag giving personal information to the potential recipient. Upon completion, the filled bags were boxed together, and mailed overseas.

This seemingly simple act of Girl Scouts "helping others" resulted in my first letter from Stella in May, 1946. What a delightful surprise! Dr. Richard Van Praagh described it in a much more dramatic fashion: "And you were contacted by Stella, rising like Phoenix from the ashes of the worst war in the history of the world!"

*Girl Scout members in San Augustine, 1945-46, included Laquita Ledford, Paula Whitton, Evva Dene Johnson, Gwendolyn Hall, Jane Teel Youngblood, Frances Bussey, Martha Sweet, Rosemary Mathews, Jean Cartwright, Jeanette Gellatly, Pat Mathews, Sarah Pearce, and Betty Wood.

CHAPTER FOUR

"Letters from Stella" 1946–1956

$\mathcal{O}$ ver a ten year period Stella Zacharioudakis and I exchanged many more letters than the sixteen that were saved. I have my mother, Anna Fay Wood, to thank for safe-keeping these treasured correspondences for me. During my college years, 1951 to 1955, Stella and I kept in touch, and I regret that many of those letters were lost in moving back and forth between the University of Texas at Austin and San Augustine. The letters we exchanged over the years were all handwritten. They are carefully transcribed with Stella's exact wording.

The first letter I received from Stella was in response to the Girl Scout gift bag sent overseas in early 1946. I suppose we will never know how the package of collected bags from our troop found its way to Rethymno, Crete.

Stella's "thank you" correspondence pictured a young girl and campfire, with tents in the background, likely an identifying reminder of the world wide connection in the Girl Scouts organization.

COVER OF FIRST LETTER FROM STELLA WITH
"BEST WISHES" GREETING, TIED WITH COLORED STRING

Rethymno
5-12-1946

My dear friend,

I am very glad to say that I have received from you a little sac with useful gifts. I thank you very much. Now I prepare a small pack from different products of my country to send you. I hope that you will receive it after some days.

I am a little girl. I am twelve years old and I live in a little town near the sea. I lived very happy but three months ago my father was dead suddenly. Now I am very unfortunate because my father was merchant, and after his death we lost all our property. Happily living some hours near my friends girl scouts I forget a little my great misery.

I am waiting for a letter from you. I will be very glad if you like to continue our correspondence. I desire very much to learn many things about your life. I wish you happy Christmas day and also a happy new year.

Excuse for my mistakes but only before six months I began to learn English.

I embrasse you,*
Stella Zacharioudakis

*Stella's 'embrasse' is the French way of spelling "embrace." She was fluent in French, which was the favored language of European diplomacy at that time, i.e., before World War II and in the years following.

A PEN AND INK SKETCH SIGNIFYING GIRL SCOUTING,
TIED WITH STRING.

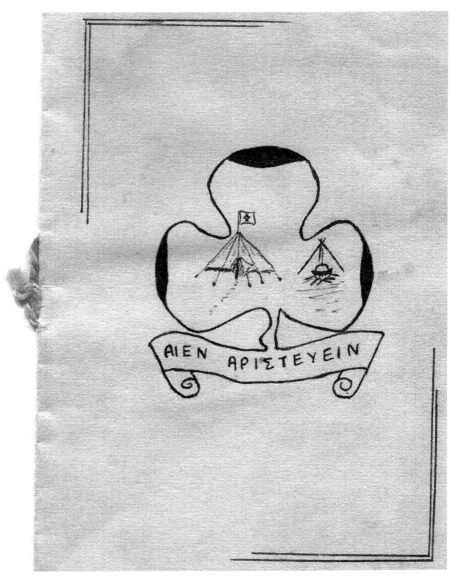

Athens
1-3-1947

Dear Betty,

I received your letter some days ago. Now I live in Athens in my uncle's house. So your letter who arrived at first at Rethymno was overdue and came to me a little late.

But when I received it I felt a great joy. You are very kind to send me the picture of you and of your little sister also. Now I see them and I think that you are near to me. Your little sister is a full of charm girl and I pray you to give her some kiss from me.

I also enclosed a picture of me. I read your letter to my friends and I gave them the addresses of your schoolfellows. I hope that very soon your friends will receive their letters.

Now in Athens I continue going to the girls scouts. The spring came to our country. The nature full of beauty wait for us. I'll be really glad if we make some excursions in the present time.

Dear Betty, I will make you a question. I pray you to tell me who is the origin of the word "naylon." All the world speak now for this matter. So I shall be eager to your answer. Write me also for your town, your school, and your life. Write me so much that you can. Because each of your letters is a great joy and a little English lesson for me.

I am very sorry that you have not received my small package. I am afraid that it is lost, but perhaps it travel soon to you. Give my greetings to the girls of your class.

All my love,
Stella

Stella's question, asking the origin of the word "nay-lon" probably referred to the new word, "nylon," a synthetic fiber invented by researchers for the DuPont Company in an attempt to find a substitute for silk. It was introduced by DuPont in 1939 during the New York World's Fair. "Nylon was first used for fishing line, surgical sutures, and toothbrush bristles. DuPont touted its new fiber as being 'strong as steel, as fine as a spider web.' The first year on the market, DuPont sold 64 million pairs of stockings. That same year, nylon appeared in the movie, The Wizard of Oz, where it was used to create the tornado that carried Dorothy to the Emerald City. In 1942, nylon went to war in the form of parachutes and tents."[6]

I have no idea as to what my answer to Stella's inquiry would have been in 1947. Back then we didn't have the "instant knowledge" of the internet. Hopefully I gave a suitable reply! In her following letter, she seemed to be satisfied with my answer.

COVER OF LETTER SHOWING COLORED SKETCH OF WINDMILL

Athens Greece
June 8, 1947

Dear Betty,

I received your letter three days ago. I am surprised at see that was send from you before a so long time. Perhaps the accidents in your country was the cause for this delay. I hope that your town is far enough from Texas City and she had not suffer any destruction.

Now I will write you for my life. I think you will be surprised if I tell you that I am a student. If I tell you that I am eighteen years old and I go to the University to become doctor.

In my first letter I write you that I am the same age as yours. That is not? And now after eight months I grew some years. What a great liar! You can think, Betty. Oh no, I like say always the true. My false age in the first letter was a guiltless lie which helped the beginning of our correspondence. I thought that never you would write in a girl so greater than you.

Now that I know you from your letters and your photo, now that I feel a great love of you, Betty. I am sure that you continue write me although my age is eighteen years.

My lessons in the University are very interesting. Some days ago the lessons of this year are finished but we continue in the summer our practical lessons in studio. We are study very small subjects with the microscope. After it we will make lessons of anatomy in the corpse of some animals, insects, and birds. Also now we are study the human skeleton and I have one at home.

All these are not horrible for us because we think that will be the means to arrive at our great aim: to become good doctors. Enough about school.

Betty I thank you for your answer in my question. Now I please you to write me if my letters are very comic so that I know a little your language. I hope that the next winter I will be able to study English enough and then I'll write you better. You asked me to tell you what is the date of my birth to send me some small gift. Thank you Betty. Unhappily my birth day is passed for this year. Is the 18 Mars. You can wait for a small gift from me on your birthday.

I enclose today a photo in which I am with my best friend in the University. I hope you could know me because is only three months later than the other that I have send you.

I am waiting for a letter from you.

All my love
Stella.

P.S.
My friend's name is Cybele. She know also a little English and is really glad when I give her learn your letters. Now she sends you love and greetings.

In reference to Stella's mention of the Texas City disaster in her letter dated June 8, 1947, I continue to be amazed that she had heard of this deadliest and worst industrial accident in American history less than two months after it occurred on April 16, 1947. "Originating with a mid-morning fire on board the French-registered vessel *SS Grandcamp* docked in the port of Texas City, its cargo of approximately 2,300 tons of ammonium nitrate detonated, with the initial blast and subsequent chain-reaction of further fires and explosions in other ships and nearby oil storage facilities killing at least 581 people, including all but one of the Texas City

Fire Department. More than 5,000 persons were injured, and property damage was estimated at $100 million (in today's terms, $1.06 billion)."[7]   San Augustine, being located about 170 miles from Texas City, was not directly affected, although a number of people from our area were involved.

PHOTO OF STELLA AND CYBELE AT THE UNIVERSITY

Athens
28-7-1947

Dear Betty

I received your letter some days ago. Excuse me that only today I answer you, but I have difficult lessons to do so that my free hours are not many. Betty you are very kind to write me so great a letter. I thank you very much. I hope that now after you know my true age you will continue to write me. I am really glad when I receive a letter from you. When I hold the leaf of Texas tree in my hand I think that the little Betty and all her lovely country are near me. Your life Betty is very happy and important. I bless you that you can learn drive the car. In our country we have not the occasion to enjoy with so interesting things. But we have a nice cloudless sky and a calm (in the summer) blue sea in which we are going to swim with my friend Cybele when we have not lessons.

I think you will be surprised to read in my letter that we continue our lessons in summer also. This it is not happened each year. Only this year that a disorder in winter prevent us to finish our lessons in the different laboratories.

Betty I enclose you today a small branch of Acropolis' olive tree.* Would you like to tell you the history of this tree? There is happened many years ago—perhaps 2500 years ago. The antiques habitans of Greece. They have not a god but twelve. I think you must know some of them. They were Jupiter, Diana, Minerva, Venus, Juno, Neptune, Mercury, Mars, Ceres, Apollo, Pluto, Vulcan.** Two of them, Minerva (goddess of the wisdom) and Neptune (god of the sea) they made angry because they would the one and the other to have *in their patronage the town of Athens. At last they agree to give a gift to the town, and he who will give the better, he have the town in his protection. Then the Neptune beat the ground with his trident, and they was appearing two fine horses. After Minerva beat also the ground with her lance, and it was grow a great olive tree. Jupiter who was the judge of the contest said that the better gift was the Minerva's olive tree. So Minerva became the goddess of the town of Athens (Minerva in Greek = Athina). This is a fable in which is hidden a great truth. The olive tree symbolizes the tranquil pacific life instead of the horses which symbolize a life of alarm and trouble. So for the peaceful ancients Athenians the Minerva's gift was the better. I hope to understand this story although I have innumerable syntax mistakes.*

You would find also in my letter a photo of the Parthenon, the Minerva's temple which unfortunately has suffered many ruins. But and now is very beautiful. I am really happy when I sit down near to his columns. All around they appear so clear and full of light from there. I have much speak for my country. That is not? You are not wearied Betty?

Dear Betty. I thank you for your wish to send me a present of your country. Excuse me if I refuse your offer. I would not Betty to make for me a so great pain. My little cousin Maria Gerakari has written to your friend Paula Whitton. Received she this letter? Betty I can not understand the name of the girl from Rethymno who write to your friend Martha. Write me her name and I will tell you if I know her.

My friend Cybele wish to correspond with an American girl. If one of your friends wish the same write to the address: Cybele Papadopoulou, Lysimahou ii Pagrati, Athens—Greece.

Betty I have not understand which is the letter that it was lost? I have receive from you three letters. Have you send me more? I would to write you other things but I must finish. Send me if you will one of the drawings that you have drawn. I am interested of drawing but I can not draw well. I think Betty about coming to the USA and I wish this very much but after I have finish the lessons of the Greek University. Give my love to your family.

With all my love,
Stella

AN OLIVE TREE IN GREECE. PHOTO BY JOHN OGLESBEE

*Dr. Richard Van Praagh explained the informative narrative given by Stella in her letter dated 28-7-1947 as follows: "Stella is telling you the history of an olive tree from the Acropolis of Athens, where the Parthenon is located. As you know, in ancient cities, the citadel (defensive fortress) was typically located at the highest point in the city: *acro*, highest point or summit; *polis*, city (Greek). The highest point in a city was the easiest to defend. Why? Because attacking up a hill is much more difficult than attacking on the level, or attacking downhill. Our aphorism, "It was an uphill battle" reflects this ancient understanding. Defending against attackers who had to climb up a steep hill was the best defensive position. From the top of a hill, defenders could roll huge boulders down on the attackers, or they could pour boiling oil on the attackers. Arrows and javelins are much harder to defend against if they are raining down from above. Attackers would have to try to hold their shields over their heads, and could not use cavalry or battering rams against an acropolis. Stella is trying to say that this olive tree is thought to be 2500 years old, dating from about 500 BC. This is all true. Recognizing that this olive tree is older than Christianity, Stella is trying to tell you about the gods of the ancient Greeks. Dear Stella also tells you the wonderful tale of the contest between Athena, the goddess of wisdom, and Poseidon, god of the sea, with Zeus as the judge. Athena (wisdom) wins over Poseidon (the sea). What a splendidly Greek allegory this is. Wisdom trumps trade. The Greeks played a very major role in the development of science. And they were also great maritime traders, as were the Phoenicians. The Greeks and the Phoenicians were collaborators in maritime trade, which they did all around the Mediterranean Sea. So Athena and Poseidon were metaphors for two of the greatest desires of the ancient Greek world—the desires for wisdom and wealth. The ancient Greeks chose wisdom as their highest value. Dear Stella was also telling you why the Hellenes named their capital city after Athena, the goddess of wisdom."

Dr. Richard continued, "It is thought that the alphabet was invented only once, by the Phoenicians of Ugarit who invented the consonants, and later by the Greeks who added the vowels. The Greeks and the Phoenicians were trading together. They established a base on a little island close to Naples (Neapoli—New Town, in Greek). It is thought that it was the Greek children who invented the vowels, while playing with the Phoenician children. Instead of using the diacritical marks to suggest the vowels, as the Phoenicians had been doing, the Greek children added the vowels that were clearer and easier to understand. And so, what we call the Greek alphabet was born. It was modified by the Romans much later, and this is now 'our' alphabet. So, Poseidon was no mean competitor. The needs of trade led to the alphabet, which in turn facilitated the development of science.

Dr. Van Praagh concluded his remarks as follows: "Socrates, Plato, and Aristotle were the ancient Greek academic trinity. Socrates argued that virtue is knowledge, and that vice is ignorance. Although condemned to death by his fellow Athenians for corrupting the minds of the young, Socrates died in the presence of his students, still professing the great value of knowledge and the profound dangers of ignorance. For the great benefit of the young, Socrates was, in fact, pointing the way to the modern world. Dear Stella was both a philosopher and a scientist. As you discovered, Stella was living proof that the ancient Greek enlightenment lives on, now illuminating most of the world today." *(from Dr. Van Praagh's letter dated September 7, 2014)*

**Stella listed the twelve primary gods in Greek mythology with the more familiar Roman names. This terminology was not surprising, in that she was attempting to be as clear as possible with her descriptions as she enlightened me on the subject. Thus, Zeus was Jupiter, Hera was Juno, Artemis was Diana, Apollon (or later, Helios) was Apollo, Demeter was Ceres, Athena was Minerva, Hermes was Mercury, Poseidon was Neptune, Ares was Mars, Hades was Pluto, Aphrodite was Venus, and Hephaestus was Vulcan.

THE PARTHENON, PHOTO BY JOHN OGLESBEE

Athens
25-8-1947

Dear Betty

I received your letter some days ago. I am glad that my age is not an obstacle to continue our correspondence. I hope you have received my last letter with the little bunch from the Minerva's olive tree. After a few days you will celebrate your birthday. I want so much to send you a gift from the Greece. So I have prepared a small package into which they were enclosed two vases of the Greek pottery. I am going to the post—full of joy—to send you this. But there they said me that it is forbit to send anything to foreign country. I was really sorry this moment Betty. Now I send you into my letter a very small gift: a bracelet from a show of Greek handmade silver work. I will be very glad if you receive it and if you like of it.

Cybele (Kiveli in Greek) is very happy that your cousin wish to write her. You have probably received my letter in which you can find her address. Now she is waiting for a letter from your cousin. She would write firstly but she think that is more easy to your cousin to make the beginning of their correspondence. You write in your own language. So you can write anything you think. But for us this is difficult enough. I should wish to write you so many things for my life and my thoughts about the life. I should wish to ask you so many questions about the reflections that you have for all things in the world. But it is so difficult now that I know so bad your language. For this I please you excuse me if my letters are not interesting.

Now I am study hard for the examins that I must pass in October. After them if I succeed, I will begin the second year of the medicine science. All the years are six. Our lessons of the first year are Botanique, Chemistry, Zoology, Physics and study of the human skeleton. They are all very interesting so that I am glad to study them. Are you interested for a lesson more than the others who you learn in the school? Are you like for books? I am very much. The books are for me very good friends. Perhaps the best friends.

Betty excuse me for the greasy spot which you will find in this page of my letter. My little cat has jumped up and make it with her dirty foot. It is not kind to send you this letter but now I have not the time to write another. Excuse me please.

Give all my love to your parents and your little sister.

Lots of love
Stella

Athens
14-9-1947

Dear Betty

I received your letter a few days ago. I am really glad to learn that my last letter with the bracelet arrived on the day before your birthday. Oh Betty you are very kind to find it so beautiful. I thank you for it. The flowers that you have draw for me in your last letter they are so fine! I assure you, you draw better than me. So I please you, if you like it, continue to draw in each of your letters something for me. I will make the same for you too. In the first page of my letter you will find some wonderful animals so that I have see them with the microscope. Can you think Betty that they are animals those little existences which seem as flowers? Their name in the universal nomination is "vorticella nebulifera." Their body is only a cellule and they live into the water. Perhaps you have hear of them in the school.

Also write me for a book that you are interested. I wish to exchange books as we do letters. If you will I can send you too a series of pictures from the different ancients and new monuments of Athens. You can send me if it not difficult a book of Jean Webster with the heading "Daddy long legs." I have learned it in a Greek translation and I wish to learn it also in English. And I please you again to send me this, only if it is not difficult for you. I think now you will have begun to go to school. So I hope you will write me in your next letter the news of your school life.

My dear Betty why you will so much to send me something from your country? Are you sure that it is not a pain for you? If indeed you would give this a great pleasure send me what you will. I like all the things in the world and I prefer the school's objects. So I would to have an American stylographe.

Betty do you like the puzzles? I write you some of those that I know. "Why is the letter 'p' like a selfish friend? Because it is first in 'pity' and last in 'help'."

"What is the queerest animal living? An author, because his tale (tail) comes out of his head."

Write me also if you know some.

Give my love to all your family and your friend Paula who has written a very nice letter to my cousin Mary.

Lots of love,
Stella

POSTCARD SHOWING JUPITER'S TEMPLE

ΝΑΟΣ ΟΛΥΜΠΙΟΥ ΔΙΟΣ   ΑΘΗΝΑΙ   TEMPLE DE JUPITER

Athens
28 October 1947

Dearest Betty

I received your letter a few days ago. Excuse me I answer you today only. But now I pass my examins in the University. I have lots of lessons to do. I have not received the fountain pen you send and the book that you have send me. But I hope I will receive them soon. Cybele received a letter from your cousin and she is very happy for.***

Lots of love
Stella

***My first cousin Hazel Faye Sanders wrote to Stella's friend Cybele for quite some time. Hazel believes Cybele became a doctor, married a doctor, and lives (or lived) in England.

Athens, Greece
December 22, 1947

Dear Betty,

I have received your letter and your wishes for Christmas in the past week, so I will answer both of them at the same time. I thank you for the picture that you sent me. It likes me very much and I believe for a moment that you are near me Betty. Also, I thank you so much for your wishes for Christmas and the new year.

We also celebrate Christmas and the first day of the new year, and we do it as you. But we receive the more gifts from parents and friends at the first day of the new year and not at Christmas. We do also for this day the royal cake. We put into this cake a silver or a gold coin and we believe for great luck to be this coin into our piece of cake. We cut the royal cake at twelve o'clock justly when the new year commences. Write me please if you have also those customs.

Now we have stopped to go to University. Each year and this year also we have two weeks Christmas vacation.

Would you like to write you how I am getting along in the University. I do it with pleasure.

I passed well my examins and now I am in the second year of the medicine science. Our lessons now are more difficult and more interesting.

They are the lesson of Anatomy the lesson of Physiologie and the lesson of Chemistry organique. We

*study now the human body on reals human corpses.
Perhaps you think that it is terrific but I assure you it
is not at all. It is very interesting to discover the arter-
ies the veins and the nerves under the skin and the
muscles. We do it into a great parlor which has two
of her walls full of windows. There are 29 corpses on
29 special tables and all around them 300 studying
students. Cybele's table and mine are justly opposite.
We are very glad for it. She also is happy to correspond
with your cousin.*

*Unfortunately I have not received even your pack-
age. So I am afraid that it has been lost in the mail.
For I pray you don't send me something in the future
because perhaps it will be lost also.*

*Enclosed you will find a picture of stadium and
another of the national library in Athens.*

*In each of my letters I will send you some like them,
pictures to know Athens.*

Can you do it for San Augustine your town?

*Please write me soon. Your letters are always wel-
come here.*

With all my love
Stella

Athens, Greece
January 13, 1948

Dear Betty,

*I received today your package. I am very glad and I
thank you as much as I can. The hose, the fountain
pen, the book, and the "crayon," all are so fine! I am
proud to have a so kind friend as you. My letter today*

is written with the fountain pen that you sent me, and which will be my lovely object by now. It is a great service for me so can write with ink wherever that I will be.

I will try to read the story of Cherry Ames as soon as I can, although I think it will not be very easy for me. Her picture is very sympathetic and seems to tell me "My life is simple and full of courage, try to know me."

Enclosed you will find a little silver knife which you can use as a jewel. It is a charming imitation of the knife that they used as an arm some years ago the habitants of my island Crete. I will be happy if it likes you.

I wish so much to send you and other things of my country but is forbit to send you a package. It is permit to send to foreign country only books. But can you read the Greek books?

Now the weather in Athens is warm enough. The sky is almost all the days clear and the sunlight give me a great joy. Till now, the winter is my light and I am happy for this. I love the snow—perhaps because I have never seen in my life—but I don't like cold weather.

Betty, like you literature and music? I am very interested in both of them. Unfortunately now I have not the time to be occupied with them. I hope in future—when I will be a doctor—to have some hours out of work and lessons to read the fine and very interesting books of the greatest authors.

Betty write me please for a book that you would wish to have. Perhaps I can find it here and I'll be glad to send it to you.

You will find also into my letter near the little knife a small flower. It is the flower of an almond tree. I *don't know if you have in Texas this tree. It is the tree which is full of flowers when all the others have not one. Its fruit is used as food by many manners. I love very much the almond trees when they are full of flowers. It seems to tell to me that the winter almost had gone and that the Spring will come soon.*

Please write me soon and tell me all your news. Give my love to all of your family.

With all my love
Stella

STELLA STUDYING, UNIVERSITY OF ATHENS MEDICAL SCHOOL, 1948

Athens
10 March 1948

Dear Betty

I have received your letter many days ago. Excuse me I answer you just now. I had lots of lessons to do this time. I hope you do not think I have forgotten you for I certainly have not.

I thank you very much for the description of your school life. I am always interested about it. I know your athletic games except soccer. We do not play this game here but I think it will be interesting.

I like all the athletic games and sports too, but now I have not time to enjoy with them.

I thank you so much for your attempt to make for me some postcards of the main sights of San Augustine.

I will have the chance to tell you if you are a good photographer.

Unhappily I do not have a camera so I can't send you but postcards.

Enclosed you will find a band for your books. You will put it into the page that you are reading. On the one extremity of this band is hand-(tied) a little shoe like the shoes that wore some Greek soldiers in the past time. Even today the men of the guard of the "unknown soldier" wear shoes like this. We call them: tsacouchia. Can you pronounce this word? Pronounce it as it is written.

These soldiers also wear a charming dress. You can see it in the postcard that I send you. Also you will find enclosed a small bunch of a flower that we name as you pronounce the word "frases." Did you

*have this flower in Texas? Here now bloom many of
these flowers no in the fields but in the gardens. They
are very lovely to me for they have a very agreeable
perfume.*

*Now that I write you the sun shines in a clear sky.
The swallows are coming and the Spring too. I am so
glad for it.*

*My lessons in the University are always interesting
and I am pleased to learn them.*

*Cybele is even my best friend and she is very glad
for the greetings that you send her. She also send you
her best wishes.*

*She has received a very charming picture from your
cousin Hazel.*

*At last I beg your pardon again and I please you to
write me soon.*

Greetings to your family
I love you lots
Stella

The flower Stella mentioned is freesia. Unbelievably, after nearly fifty years in the envelope with the letter above, the little dried spray was still in one piece, with its curved head and tiny trumpet-shaped blossoms intact, and immediately recognizable.

In the early lines of the letter dated 10 March 1948 Stella indicated that she did not know of the game of soccer. Dr. Richard Van Praagh reminded me that "In Greece and all over Europe the game is called football. Soccer is our name for European football, to distinguish it from American football."

Athens Greece
May 7, 1948

Dear Betty

I received your letter many days ago. I did not answered you sooner because I would to find the stamps that you demanded me.

I have never do a collection of stamps, but I thought that my brother had one. So I wrote to him (he remains in Rethymno) and he send me some from his collection. Enclosed you will find them. I had explain to your language what represents each of the stamps. I think it will be interesting for you to learn the meaning of them. Some of the stamps are published before the last war (I have marked them with a red cross). Some others during the war and some after the war (I marked them with a green cross). I hope you are like of them. Enclosed you will find also some stamps whose we use now for exchange them with your friends. In future I will try to find and others to send you.

The past Sunday we celebrated the Easter the greatest feast for the people of Greece. We have many interesting customs for the day.

My news from the University are always well. Now approach the time of the examinations, so I have much work to do. This is the reason that my letter is short today and written in haste.

Give my greetings to your family and friends.

All my love
Stella

The assortment of stamps Stella sent from Greece were added to the large brown hard-cover book containing "Stamps of the World," which I kept for years, then passed on for the enjoyment of our children. Looking back, I can't believe that I would have been presumptuous enough to make such a request! She was certainly thoughtful in asking her brother to help her, but it had to be trouble for both of them. I hope I thanked her profusely!

Rethymno
i Augustus 1948

Dear Betty

I received your letter some time ago. Now I remain in Rethymno and I plan to stay here until October when the University will be starting. In Crete the weather is very agreeable and it's not pretty hot as in Athens.

The sea is very near to our house so I go every day in swimming. Next week we will go to our little farme to stay the rest summertime. I hope that I will have many interesting things to do there, as to visit the neighboring villages, to take part in the vintage of our vineyard, to read interesting books under the shadow of the trees.

I like very much the life in the fields of my country. Don't you?

I thank you so much for the beautiful remembrance which you sent me for my birthday.

Also I thank you for the stamps you have enclosed in your letter. I gave them to my brother who has a collection of stamps. He thinks also that stamp collecting

is an interesting hobby but I have not the same opin-
ion. So he sent you some other stamps from different
countries and you will find them enclosing with my
letter.

I hope that when you will receive my letter you will
have returned from your trip to Carlsbad and Mexico.
You will be very kind if you write me in your next letter
your impressions from this trip.

Did you write any time to your cousin Hazel? If
you do it I please you to write her that my friend Cybele
has not receive any letter from her many days ago.
Cybele wish always to correspond with Hazel and she
can't understand her silence. Please write me soon your
news.

With all my love
Stella

The vacation Stella mentions was one my parents, sister
and I took to Colorado and Carlsbad Caverns in New Mexico
during the summer of 1948. I remember purchasing postcards of the places we visited, both for keepsakes and to send
Stella when we returned home.

Hazel's mother passed away after a long illness during the
late 1940s. Hazel lived with our grandmother in the years
following, and often spent summers with my family in San
Augustine. Hazel and Cybele continued their correspondence some time later.

"The Church of our Lady in Dafni"

the church of our Lady in Dafni

> *Rethymno*
> *24-8-48*

Dearest Betty

> *Many happy returns of*
> *The day and all my love*
> > *Stella*

I am sending you (some days ago) for your birthday a package with a manufacture made in my island Crete. I hope you can use it like an excursion bag as we do here or for what you like. I will be very happy if it like you.

Send me please your next letter in Athens because after some days I will be there.

> *With my love*
> *Stella*

The church in this postcard is a very old and famous church for his sacred images. Dafni is a village near of Athens.

೪

Rethymno
8-8-49

Dear Betty

I received your letter many days ago. I am very sorry that I could not answer you sooner but I hope you will forgive me. When I received your letter I was very busy in the University.

After I am going away from Athens and now I remain in Rethymno my native town. I am very glad to be again in my paternal house near to my mother. The sea is very near to our house so that each day I go to swim with my friends. One of them passed the last winter in the United States in the University of Mississippi and now she can tell to me many things for your country and your life in school.

You will find enclosed in my letter two pictures of me. In the largest of them I am with some of my fellow students after a surgery lesson. I marked myself with a little cross.

Today I am sending your birthday present. I hope to receive it soon since I'll send it by air mail. I'll be very glad if you find lovely the "jupe" and the little money box made the two also in Crete.

The present you send to me for my birthday is not reached even in Athens.

I write you short letters because I don't know well your language. I hope in future to be able to write you better.

Please write me soon. I'll stay in Rethymno till the end of September.

Lots of love
Stella

STELLA AND FELLOW STUDENTS AFTER A SURGERY LESSON. SHE IS
SECOND FROM LEFT, KNEELING.

(SKETCH OF LITTLE GREEK MAN, TREE, SHIP, AND WORD ON SCROLL
"KENTN" ON COVER)

STELLA'S CHRISTMAS GREETINGS WERE
INSIDE THIS FOLDED NOTE CARD.

23-12-49

To dear Betty

Merry Christmas
and
a Happy New Year

Stella

Athens Greece
June 20, 1950

Dear Betty

*I have received your letter today. I am really ashamed
to have no writing to you in a so long time.*

*Please forgive me and don't think that I forget you.
A serious sickness who obliged my sister to rest in bed
four months and the many lessons whose had to follow
in University make me incapable to occupied with my
friends. Now my sister is almost well and the University
has been out. So I can write you again. I can go to sea
for swimming, I can do excursions to our mountains.
It is really fun to swim in the ocean because we enjoy
very much playing with the waves whose arrive full of
foam.*

*But it is also a little dangerous because sometimes
a man-eater fish can be appeared. Last summer a boy
17 years old has a very terrible death by such one fish.*

*This summer I will not go to Crete. I must stay in
Athens to study some of my lessons that I left for the
autumnal examination time.*

*We have also here very hot weather who is a bad
partner for my study. I envy you that you can spend
your time so fine and without cares of lessons.*

*Enclosed you will find a picture of me. It is made
some months ago in one excursion to a low mountain
near Athens. The other boys and girls are some of my
student fellow. In this excursion the snow has given
me some of the greatest pleasures of my life. I hope you
will be able to recognize me. A little arrow will help
you. I will be very glad if you also send me a new picture of you as soon as you have one.*

Please don't be late as I to answering to my letter. I like so much to have your news.

Lots of love
Stella

Stella graduated from the University of Athens, School of Medicine, Athens, Greece in 1952. During the years 1953-54 she was External Assistant, Children's Hospital of Athens University, Greece. Stella was in the United States during the years 1954-1955 as a Rotating Intern at Christ Hospital, Jersey City, New Jersey. Her presence in America provided an opportunity for my family to invite her to spend Christmas 1954 with us in San Augustine. Her letter dated December 8, 1954 follows:

Dearest Betty

I felt so guilty yesterday when I received your letter. Long ago I wanted to write you and I always postponed the main reason is still my difficulty to express myself in English. If you could understand Greek sweet Betty! I should have so many things to write to you. Let us hope that my English will be improving so that I will not have later a really hard time when I want to write to you.

Although late enough I will tell you about my visit to Niagara Falls. It is really something wonderful and the strength of the nature is there expressed with one of the nicest way. You can stay and look at this tremendous amount of falling water for hours and hours and you don't get tired. The rainbows that are formed over the surface of the river and the white foam of the falling water complete with their color the beautiful picture.

What I didn't like was the touristic environment of this natural beauty. I believe—and maybe I am wrong—that the tendency to make money out of every kind of natural beauty is one of the biggest defect of our modern life. I should be very happy if I could see Niagara Falls with their wildness with a small company of good friends without the thousands of tourists who make so much noise around you, without the elevators who bring you nearer to the river, without the postcards and the souvenirs that appear in every place on your way to the falls. I know I want something impossible. But still I don't like to change my desires and my way of thinking.

Maybe the reason is way back in my childhood which offered me the natural beauty and serenity with a completely different way during my summer vacation in the small villages of Crete.

I like to believe that also in U.S. there are places with simple quiet people and less artificial life and where the kindness of that people make unimportant every lack of the high convenience which you find in the big cities. I have read that the south part of U.S. is a place similar to Europe.

Your friendship, your letters and all the way that you treat me is the best prove that I have.

Your mother's letter today gave me all the warmth and the kindness of your hospitality. I feel awfully sorry that I will not be able to visit you during Christmas time. My time off during Christmas is only 36 hours. From 12 p.m. Saturday to 8 a.m. Monday. And besides, 8 days later in the 1st of January I have to leave for Buffalo where I am going to be for my residency in Pediatrics. (I have already an appointment in the Children's Hospital of Buffalo University.)

I have to prepare several things before I leave and is not so easy to do at this same time a long trip to Texas. But I promise that next summer I will find the way to meet you.

I am so anxious to meet you and all your family and stay with you a few days. And also—who knows? It is very possible that you may come to New York or to Niagara Falls or to have together a trip during summer and enjoy together some days of our vacations. Let us hope in the future since the present doesn't offer many opportunities to see each other.

Now I must close. I want to thank your mother so much for her letter and her invitation, and for the picture of you that she sent to me, which I like more than any other you have sent to me. It should be a great request if I ask a picture of all your family as soon as you have one? I love to have it.

I hope you don't find much difficulty to understand my poor English. I will write again to you soon, probably when I am going to leave for Buffalo. Your letters are a happiness for me. Don't forget to send them to me as often as possible.

> *Lots of love to all of you and all my thanks for your invitation.*
> *Stella*

P.S.
I send to your mother the picture you find in this letter. I didn't have any better. It is taken in the garden of the hospital. The others are doctors and nurses of the hospital.

STELLA ON FRONT ROW WITH GROUP OF DOCTORS AND NURSES.

Stella's Easter greetings to me and my family were sent from Children's Hospital in Buffalo, New York in April, 1955. The simple message inside a lovely card said:

To dearest Betty
and all her family
my best wishes for
a very happy Easter
Lots of love
Stella April 6, 1955

Although Stella was unable to spend Christmas in 1954 with my family, 1955 was a different story. Once again my mother invited her to spend the Christmas holidays with us, and this time her schedule allowed her to come.

I had graduated from the University of Texas at Austin in May 1955, and was teaching first grade in Port Arthur, Texas for the current school year. At home in San Augustine for the holiday season, I joined my family in preparing for Stella's visit with great anticipation. Aunts, uncles, cousins, and grandparents had been invited to our home for Christmas dinner, and everyone knew Stella was coming. We could hardly wait!

Having a new teaching position made possible the purchase of my first car, a small Ford sedan. My mother Anna Fay, my sister Leslie, and I drove to the Shreveport, Louisiana airport to meet Stella's flight.   Ninety miles from San Augustine, Shreveport had the most convenient airport for her arrival.

Ten eventful years had passed since Stella and I had begun our correspondence and friendship. As she walked toward us, smiling in her relaxed and pleasant manner, I was thinking, "Here is my wonderful, brilliant friend. She has overcome unbelievable challenges in her life, maintaining through it all a genuine empathy for the feelings of others, and now she is clearly in the midst of reaching her goals.   We are not strangers. I have known her forever, and we are finally meeting face to face."

At the immature age of twelve, living a somewhat sheltered life in America and rural Eastern Texas, I could not possibly comprehend the magnitude of what Stella had overcome to arrive at the point in life where her dreams were coming to fruition. But as a young adult, in the airport that day in December 1955, I understood, without saying a word.

Stella's days with my family went quickly, with never a dull moment. She was the perfect house guest, always complimentary and appreciative at each meal and for every favor that came her way. She seemed to enjoy the peas, cornbread, and sweet potatoes of our daily meals, as well as the turkey and dressing at Christmas dinner. Perhaps her "Thank You" letter to my parents, written from Children's Hospital, Buffalo, New York, says it best:

January 8, 1956

Dearest Mrs. and Mr. Wood and Leslie,

I wanted to write to you from the first day I arrived in Buffalo but if you think that I am on duty every day and every other night you will understand why it took me so long to write to you, and I hope that you will forgive me.

I feel that with my poor English I will not be able to express to you how much I appreciated your hospitality and the peaceful pleasant Christmas you offered me. I am so glad that Betty has so wonderful parents as you and I also think that you are very lucky parents having Betty and Leslie as your children. Believe me I felt so easily like home in your house and I liked so much all of you that I already feel like I have met you years and years ago. San Augustine and the whole Wood family from Grand-daddy* to the little Sandy** are already very present and beloved memories in my life.

I like to hope that some other day of my life I will be able to see again at least the younger members of the family.

My stop in New York was very pleasant. I enjoyed seen some very good friends of mine and spending with them the New Year's Eve. Now back to the snow and cold of Buffalo and also back to work.

Since the 5th of January we transferred in a new beautiful building where is a pleasure really to work and the children even sick are a lot happier.

I close now because it is already late at night.

There is no need to say that I will continue to write to Betty and I will learn your news from her. I want to thank you again for your warm and sincere hospitality and I make a wish to be able to offer myself the same pleasure to Betty and Leslie in Greece.

My best greetings to all your relatives and all I met in San Augustine and to Velma.***

Sincerely yours,
Stella

*Grand-daddy was Price Wood, the oldest family member Stella met while in San Augustine.

**When Stella mentioned "Sandy," she meant Cindy Wood, the youngest child in the Wood family in 1955.

***Velma was a friend who worked part time for my mother, and assisted us in preparing Christmas dinner.

CHAPTER FIVE

The Silent Years and New Beginnings

*S*tella's and my correspondence with each other continued for a year or so after her visit to San Augustine in
December 1955. Back then, I understood that she planned to
return to Greece as a pediatrician after the completion of her
residency and medical training in the United States.

In June 1956 I married my high school and college sweet-
heart John Oglesbee. We established our home in San
Augustine, working and beginning our family. I remember
writing to Stella about the birth of our first son in November
1957. After that, our correspondence stopped.

There is no explanation for the fact that we lost touch
after so many years of writing. Perhaps multiple changes of
address for Stella over several years? Possibly a letter from
one to the other was lost in transmission. Who will ever
know what happened? Somehow, the cares and obligations
of our daily lives have a tendency to consume us. Time passes
quickly, and oftentimes years have transpired before we real-
ize it. Over those silent, intervening years, I never forgot the

unforgettable Stella. I assumed she had happily returned to her beloved homeland to practice medicine. For the next 45 years I was convinced she was in Greece.

And then, in May 2005, along came an opportunity to visit Greece. Forrest Oglesbee, our youngest son and a CPA with the Ernst and Young accounting firm, was living in Zurich, Switzerland for a few years on EY's European Team. He and his wife Sabrina invited John and me for a visit. He suggested that while there, we fly to Greece for a few days. What a delightful idea! I immediately said, "Maybe I can find Stella!"

An inquiry to our son Dr. John Oglesbee brought his response, "The last information you have about Stella is that she attended Johns Hopkins School of Medicine while in the United States. Contact their offices via the internet, perhaps they can help."

On Monday, May 2, 2005, I received a most welcome reply from Judy L. Walter, Associate Registrar, Johns Hopkins University School of Medicine in Baltimore, Maryland.

> *Ms. Betty W. Oglesbee:*
>
> *Your inquiry concerning Stella Zacharioudakis has been forwarded to me for reply.*
>
> *After she graduated from medical school, Stella Zacharioudakis completed a one year postdoctoral fellowship in the department of pediatrics at Johns Hopkins University School of Medicine. Dr. Zacharioudakis was at Hopkins from July 1957 until June 1958.*
>
> *We have no current address information for Dr. Zacharioudakis. However, upon searching the internet on Google, I have located what appears to be fairly current information for her. Her married name is Stella Van Praagh. According to a website of the Canadian Pediatric Cardiology Association, Drs. Richard and Stella Van*

Praagh have been in the Boston area since 1965. They founded and built the Cardiac Registry at Children's Hospital in Boston. I suggest you contact Children's Hospital in Boston for more current information.

In addition, there is a nice article about Drs. Richard and Stella Van Praagh at the website mentioned above.

Good luck in contacting Dr. Van Praagh and enjoy your vacation in Greece.

Sincerely,
Judy L. Walter

I quickly composed a letter to Stella, sending it in care of Children's Hospital, Boston, since this was the only address provided. I hoped it would reach her before we left for Europe.

San Augustine, Texas
May 9, 2005

Dr. Stella Zacharioudakis Van Praagh
Children's Hospital
300 Longwood Avenue
Boston, MA 02115

Dear Stella:

I'm sure you will be surprised to hear from this "voice out of the past!" It must have been at least 46 years since we corresponded. I remember writing you about the birth of my first son in November 1957. From that point I believe we lost touch, and I'm so sorry we allowed that to happen! Perhaps if there had been e-mail back then, staying in contact would have been easier.

Over these many years I've remembered you, and thought of you! My mother, Anna Fay Wood, died in December 1999. Among her memorabilia I found the "Thank You" letter you wrote after your visit with our family in San Augustine at Christmastime, 1955. I still cherish the beautiful metal box that you gave me then, although its velvet lining is long since gone. I always felt that you had returned to Greece as a pediatrician after your graduation from Johns Hopkins.

Thus, when my husband John and I planned a mid-May trip to Switzerland to visit our son Forrest and his wife Sabrina, and decided to fly to Greece for a few days with them, I determined to find you if at all possible. Our son Dr. John suggested trying in advance to locate you by contacting the Alumni Association at Johns Hopkins—a reasonably easy task with today's internet access. They referred me to the extremely helpful Registrar's office, where I was provided current information about you, including an excellent article from the Canadian Pediatric Cardiology Association. In the photograph of Drs. Richard and Stella Van Praagh accompanying the article, I recognized you immediately!

Stella! What an exciting, productive, and fulfilling life you have led! I know you must be extremely happy to have experienced such tremendous success both in your personal life and in your chosen field of pediatric medicine. I am especially impressed that you and your husband have worked with doctors in Greece, Italy, and elsewhere throughout the world with medical discoveries and techniques that improve the lives of people everywhere! The influence and outreach of both Drs. Van Praagh are truly without boundaries!

Enameled metal box from Stella, Christmas 1955.

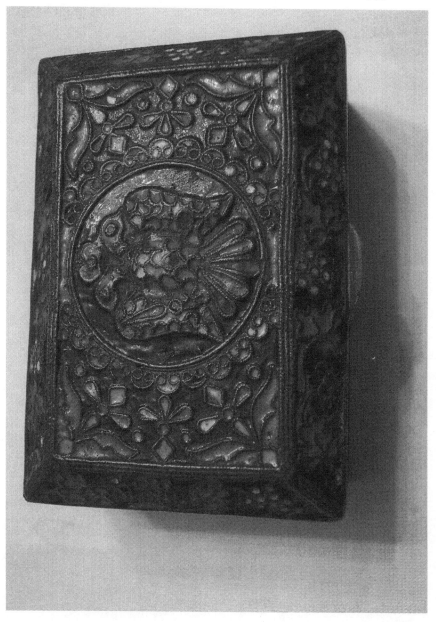

I will give you a little bit of update about my life over the years. You already know that I graduated from the University of Texas/Austin, taught school for awhile, and married John Oglesbee, also a UT graduate, in June, 1956. We have lived in San Augustine since our marriage, and are still quite involved in civic affairs, our church, historical research, and writing.

My husband's career in the Piney Woods of Deep East Texas spanned many years as a timber supplier for several area pulp and paper mills, while at the same time developing real estate properties around the nearby Sam Rayburn Reservoir.

After the children were older, I opened and operated "Heartstrings," a floral, gift, and apparel business for 35 years. I sold the store to my dear friend and long-time employee, Elizabeth McCauley, in the year 2000. Although John and I are supposedly retired, I believe we are busier than ever! We continue to do what we can to help our part of Texas prosper and grow!

John and I have four sons, all of whom are married. All four boys are graduates of the University of Texas at Austin.

Our eldest son, Dr. John Henry Oglesbee, graduated from UT's Southwestern Medical School in Dallas, and established a family practice here in San Augustine. He also serves as an Assistant Professor with UTMB in Galveston. They send third year medical students to do their family practice rotations with him. His wife Sharon is a nurse practitioner, and works with him. They have three children, two sons and a daughter.

Our second son, Vance Jackson Oglesbee, graduated from UT Pharmacy School and serves on the Board of Directors of American Pharmacies. He owns two pharmacies, in Fairfield, Texas and Corsicana, Texas. He and his wife Angela, a teacher, have two young daughters.

Our third son, James Christopher Oglesbee, is a Senior Vice-President of Bancorp South in Nacogdoches, Texas. His wife Gina is a CPA, and is Internal Auditor for Stephen F. Austin State University in Nacogdoches. They have a daughter and a son. Of interest to you would be a rather harrowing experience for our family when Chris was in 7th grade. During a routine physical, his pediatrician discovered a coarctation of his aorta. Dr. Denton Cooley performed the successful correction at Children's Hospital (St. Luke's) in Houston. Chris has had excellent health since that time.

Our fourth and youngest son, Forrest Edward Oglesbee, is a CPA with the accounting firm of Ernst and Young. He and his wife Sabrina, a speech therapist, are currently living in Zurich, Switzerland for a four-year term with his company. John and I have enjoyed two visits with them in 2003 and 2004, and we're looking forward to our trip this year, beginning May 17, 2005. For the two prior visits we have spent time in Italy, Austria and Germany in addition to most parts of Switzerland. As I mentioned, we will fly to Greece for a few days.

Stella, I would love to hear from you! Since I have only your mailing address at Children's Hospital in Boston, I decided to send this letter via US Postal Service.

Still friends...
Betty Wood Oglesbee

I did not hear from Stella before we left Texas on May 17, 2005 for Switzerland. My hope was that she had received my letter, and had not had time to respond before our flight departed. I was thrilled to find Stella's answer awaiting me when we returned home.

May 28, 2005

Dear Betty,

Your wonderful and very informative letter arrived safely at the Boston Children's Hospital some time before May 17, '05. My husband who does not go to the Hospital now every day brought it to me a few days after May 17, '05. I found your phone number from information and I called this number just to let you know that your letter had reached me. I knew that you would be in Europe by then. I hope that when you return to Texas you will find this letter waiting for you.

You and your husband have raised a wonderful family and I congratulate you both for such an achievement. I do hope that you both stay healthy to enjoy your sons and their families for many years to come.

From your letter I assume that you do have some information about my professional life. I was very fortunate to meet and marry Richard Van Praagh in June of 1962. Our marriage was the meeting of two kindred spirits. Our work in the field of Pediatric Cardiology has been creative and rewarding. We started in Toronto, Canada (Richard's home town) then in Chicago for two years and eventually in Boston at the Children's Hospital and Harvard University from 1965 to 2000. We were fortunate to see patients and to meet and teach doctors from all over the world. The Boston Children's Hospital is an important academic and therapeutic facility known to almost everybody in the field of Pediatric Cardiology. We are now both Emeritus.

My husband is writing a book, which hopefully he will be able to finish and which will include his knowledge and his experience with over 3,000 cases of various forms of congenital heart malformations. I do not have his ambition and energy and since 2002 I am fully retired from any medical activities.

We were fortunate to have three normal children. Our first son Andrew is a PhD in Molecular Microbiology and works with a pharmaceutical company which tries to produce antibiotics which are able to control very serious infections. He and his wife Cathy (also a microbiologist) have a two year old little girl.

Helen our only daughter and our second child, developed skin melanoma after the birth of her second son. She lived for five years after her diagnosis and was well for four of those five years. Then the combination of this incurable cancer and the side effects of chemotherapy gave her a very difficult year. She left us in September 2001 one week prior to 9/11. The pain from her loss will never go away, and my life will never be the same. Her two boys, now 9 and 11 years old live with their very dedicated father and we try to see them at least once a week. They live in a town 10 miles away from our own. We and their paternal grandparents can never replace what they lost. But life has to go on no matter what problems come along our way.

Our second son and third child Alexander graduated from MIT as an architect. He and his wife (who is an artist) live in Cambridge, Massachusetts and they have a year old son. We see them often since Cambridge is twenty minutes by car from Wellesley.

This is a brief account of our small family. We are thankful that at this point everybody is healthy and they are living close to us so that we can see them often.

I am well in general but I feel the aging process very definitely. My physical strength is steadily diminishing as time goes by. I am very much at peace with the idea that we are all mortals.

I am very thankful for all the happy moments that my work in this country has given me and for the joy that our children and grandchildren have provided along the way.

I do not feel eager to travel any more. Our professional life included lots of travelling to Europe, China, Japan, South America, and the USA. I feel I have seen enough of our world not to want to see more.

Helping in any way I can to improve the life of Helen's boys is my important objective at present. I wish I were stronger to do more for them.

I am touched to know that your mother saved my letter of many years ago. I also thought of you many times all those years. Yet I had realized that our worlds were very different. I assumed, probably wrongly, that you were busy and happy with your life so you could not really care about what was happening to your Greek friend who was trying to adjust and succeed in this country. I am very thankful that you made the effort to find me.

The computer age came after I could survive professionally without it. Hence I never became computer literate. By nature and by personal philosophy I do not like the dependency which the various machines bring to our lives. I feel that they destroy the beauty and the freedom of self-sufficiency.

We do not have an e-mail address. Hard to believe and yet it is true. I do hope that you will have the patience, dear Betty, to read this long hand-written "epistle." Maybe it is not inappropriate since my letter is definitely "a voice out of the past."

We have lived since 1965 in a house which was built in 1924 in Wellesley, MA. We love our house and we do not know how to face the fact that it has become bigger than what we really need. We hope to find the proper solution when we have to move.

I send you my best wishes for continuing good health and happiness and my love.

Stella.

The trip to Greece was memorable. Perfect May weather, an unbelievably beautiful Aegean Sea, roses as tall as people in full bloom everywhere, the expressive beauty of ancient, gnarled olive trees throughout the pristinely clean land-scape—words are insufficient to describe this lovely country! We realized that we barely scratched the surface of seeing Greece in the few days we were there!

In our rental car, Forrest, Sabrina, John and I traveled the entire outer edge of the Peloponnese before heading to Athens. Most highways were well marked with readable sig-nage, but occasionally we strayed from the main thorough-fare onto interior country roads with directions only in Greek. Completely lost, we would drive for miles before finding our way again. I thought of Stella, striving to learn English, and understood how difficult it must have been for her!

Stella's letter had arrived during our absence, and I could hardly wait to answer.

June 14, 2005

Dear Stella,

Thank you so much for your wonderful letter! It was waiting for me when we returned home from our trip to Greece and Switzerland. I also enjoyed hear-ing your voice on the telephone answering machine… you sounded just as I remembered you from so many years ago...your caring personality is reflected in your voice!

I really appreciate your sharing details about your family with me. I commend you and Dr. Richard for your success in raising three fine, very bright children, and for all their successes as individuals. Certainly you and your husband have set the example for them through your perseverance, brilliant dedication, and significant contributions in your chosen field of pediatric cardiology. It was a pleasure to read about your work in the biographical information provided through my contact with Johns Hopkins.

I was so very sad to learn of the loss of your daughter Helen. I think coping with losing a child would be the most difficult grief imaginable. Certainly Helen's boys will always be a reminder of her, and a comfort for you—they are her legacy! I'm glad you are able to be with them often.

Stella, I thought of you during the entire five days we were in Greece, wondering if you had received my letter, and picturing you growing up in that beautiful country. Our time in the Peloponnese and Athens were not nearly long enough. Someday we want to visit the islands and the northern part of Greece. We really enjoyed seeing the Parthenon, ancient Corinth and other archaeological sites, the spectacular scenery and mountains, and the incomparable Aegean Sea.

A highlight of our time in Greece was attending a concert during the Athens Festival in the Odeon of Herodes Atticus. On that particular cool night there were many stars, a full moon, and the lighted Parthenon as a backdrop. The music was absolutely beautiful, performed by a full orchestra, a folk orchestra, a large choir, and several soloists. Many times the audience would cheer, clap, and join in to sing along. The program was

"Mikis Theodorakis—80 years." Although we didn't understand the Greek lyrics, we thoroughly enjoyed the evening. Music is always the universal language!

We were particularly impressed with the Greek food. I purchased a Greek cookbook and have been preparing many of the salads and main dishes that we enjoyed while there. I've decided that olive oil makes everything taste better! We're hosting a meeting of John's Rotary Club in early July, and I plan to make it a "Greek Dinner Party."

I certainly understand not having e-mail or a computer. I am anything but computer literate, using mine mainly for writing. Our children are all proficient, since they use computers in education and business and basically grew up with them. If John and I have anything special to find on the computer (like looking for Stella), the boys, or the grandchildren, help us. So, it is best if you and I just continue to write "regular letters" as we did before, and leave the computers to the younger generation!

I really can't imagine how we lost touch after writing to each other for about ten years. Please let's not have that happen again! I truly believed that you had returned to Greece to practice as a pediatrician.

Just think of how much more you and your husband were able to accomplish through broadening the horizons of your medical influence! When your husband's book is published, I want to purchase a copy for our son Dr. John. Let me know when it is available.

We would be pleased to have both Doctors Van Praagh visit us in Texas! Bring Helen's boys with you, and we will enjoy having you meet the members of our family who live nearby.

I hope to hear from you soon!

Love,
Betty

I soon learned that Stella was highly acclaimed in the preparation of Greek cuisine. In the following letter, she offered to help me with the dishes for the Greek dinner party I was planning. We enjoyed several pleasant telephone conversations concerning how to succeed with the Greek recipes, although my level of expertise could never reach hers!

The hand woven embroidered table runner she sent for our upcoming Greek dinner party brought an extra dimension of interest to the evening, as I shared "The Stella Story" with our guests.

EMBROIDERED GREEK TABLE RUNNER.

June 21, 2005

Dear Betty,

I am so glad that your first visit to Greece sounds like a very pleasant one. Some of the performances of the Odeon of Herodes Atticus can be an unforgettable experience, and bring out the "Greek Soul" across the ages.

Five days is certainly not enough to see Greece. I hope that you may go back some day to see Crete (my birthplace) and some of the other islands. These islands my husband thinks, justifiably, are the farmer's nightmare and the tourist's paradise.

I am particularly pleased that you liked the Greek food and you are willing to reproduce it. You may call me anytime if you need any help when you try to follow the recipes in your book.

I am sending you a small hand woven embroidery which, I thought, you could use in one of the tables of the meeting of the Rotary Club which you are hosting in early July. It has the island of Crete on it and men and women dancing dressed in traditional costumes of the island. The border of the dancing scene is decorated with what has been called the "Greek key." I do hope that you will like it.

I would like to have, sometime, a picture of you and maybe of your family and I will try to reciprocate.

The lapse of many years in our correspondence did not affect our "pen pal" friendship. In fact, it gave time to both of us to develop and more or less to complete our life's objectives. It is an interesting story of how two young girls from two different parts of the world have become friends by exchanging letters and little else.

73

Best wishes for your health and joy this summer and always.

Love,
Stella

THE ODEON OF HERODES ATTICUS, ATHENS, GREECE

PHOTO BY JOHN OGLESBEE

June 29, 2005

Dear Betty,

Thank you very much for sending us a copy of the article which you found in the Internet about Richard and me. It is interesting to know what the Web has about our lives.

We are in Wellesley for a few days because Richard was invited to participate in the World Congress of

Cardiology and Cardiac Surgery which will take place in Buenos Aires, and he needs to be in Boston to prepare his talks. I am not going since I have been there once before and also I am fully retired from medicine.

In two days we will be returning to New Hampshire. The weather there is ideal for the summer months. I wish I could send you some of the NH cool air to make Texas temperatures more tolerable.

Congratulations for your continuing experiments with Greek cooking. I feel that your trip to Greece not only restored our friendship but also improved your cooking abilities.

I send my best wishes to all in your family and

Much love.
Stella.

THANKSGIVING CARD DRAWN BY STELLA'S DAUGHTER-IN-LAW.

October 24, 2005

Dear Betty,

It was so nice of you to call after hearing in the news of the floods in Massachusetts. Fortunately our house in Wellesley and our summer cottage in New Hampshire did not suffer any damage. This has been a year of so many natural disasters!

I thought of you many times while Katrina and Rita were devastating New Orleans and Florida. But I knew from the news which reached us that San Augustine escaped any damage. A phone call would have shown my concern although it could not really help your worries about what was happening. In retrospect I feel that I was wrong and I apologize. You always need a friendly voice to share your concerns during the times of distress even when they do not affect your directly.

My only excuse is that I am so preoccupied with the life of Helen's children that I neglect my other duties. I do hope that you understand.

I wish you and your family a very Happy Thanksgiving and hopefully an end to natural or manmade disasters.

Much love
Stella

P.S. I hope that you will like the whimsical design of my card produced by the wife of our younger son.

During the remainder of 2005 Stella and I exchanged Christmas cards and spoke on the telephone a few times. We talked again in early 2006. Then, in late summer 2006 my "letter to Stella" went unanswered. I thought, "Stella is busy with family, or vacationing, or perhaps traveling to medical meetings with her husband." I became concerned at Christmastime when there was no response to the card I sent. Then, a lovely Christmas card came, addressed in the handwriting of Dr. Richard Van Praagh.

Christmas 2006

Dear Mrs. Oglesbee,

Thank you for your beautiful Christmas card and note to dear Stella.

Alas, dear Stella died on June 3rd, 2006 following a massive stroke. It was sudden and unexpected. Dear Stella was conscious for only about 10 minutes after it happened, and in no pain. Fortunately, I was there.

We had had a beautiful day together. Sharp as a tack, and apparently well, Stella made a nice hot dinner (pasticcio) for Andrew (our elder son) and Catharine (who was full term, or perhaps a bit more) and for Abigail (3 years old). Abby loves pasticcio.

This was the last act of Stella's life.

Best Wishes,
Richard

I was shocked to hear of Stella's sudden passing. Meeting her again after so many years of silence would not happen now, and I was deeply touched and saddened at the thought. Dr. Richard Van Praagh's letter dated January 18, 2007 provided a tiny glimpse into Stella's remarkable life and career. I was most grateful to receive it.

1-18-07

Dear Mrs. Oglesbee,

Thank you very much indeed for the beautiful card, your interesting letter, and your very kind donation to the Cardiac Registry Research Fund of Children's Hospital Boston in honor of dearest Stella.

She really was a great person: a superb cardiologist, an internationally renowned research scientist, a remarkable linguist (she could read ancient Greek), and a real philosopher (she was leading an Ancient Greek Studies group here in Wellesley, fondly known as The Mythology Club). And she was so much more, besides. A remarkable cuisiniere, a radiant hostess, a role model for our young women Cardiology fellows, she was a teacher and a mother for her many students and patients alike.

You know how she would start her teaching sessions? She would start by serving everyone fresh, hot, homemade Easter bread, with lots of melted butter. In many ways, her teaching sessions were unique. Her baklava was the best that anyone had ever tasted. And she was an historian.

She would have loved your card, and your letter, and your kind gift. She would have regarded these things as your good-bye to her.

Then she might look at you and say, "Do you know what good-bye really means?"

Then she would add, "It's a contraction. It means 'God be with ye'."

Thank you,
Richard Van Praagh

While I was preparing the manuscript for _Letters from Stella_, Dr. Van Praagh was kind enough to send me a number of photographs of their family, especially of the three children, as a means of "filling in some gaps of the missing years" of my correspondence with Stella.

EASTER, 1966, THE VAN PRAAGH LIVING ROOM IN WELLESLEY, MA. (_L TO R_) ANDREW, SITTING ON KOULA, THE FAMILY'S TALENTED LIVE-IN BABY SITTER FROM GREECE; HELEN WITH STELLA, ALEX SITTING WITH GRANDMOTHER HELEN VAN PRAAGH, AND AUNT JEAN ANDERSON.

SITTING ON THE KITCHEN COUNTER, JANUARY 1968.
(*L TO R*) HELEN, ANDREW, ALEX.

APRIL, 1968. BARELY IN THE PICTURE IS NIECE CECILY VAN PRAAGH,
SITTING ON DR. RICHARD'S LAP WITH HELEN.
DR. STELLA IS HOLDING ALEX, AND ANDREW IS BESIDE HER.

DURING THE SNOWSTORM OF FEBRUARY, 1969, ON SYLVAN ROAD IN WELLESLEY, MASSACHUSETTS. *(L TO R)* ALEX, HELEN, AND ANDREW. DR. RICHARD COMMENTED, "OUR CHILDREN LOVED PLAYING IN THE SNOW, PARTICULARLY ALEX. THIS LED TO SLEDDING, TOBOGGANING, SKATING, HOCKEY, AND SKIING. DADDY AND THE CHILDREN WERE THE CRAZY OUTDOOR PEOPLE. STELLA, MY MEDITERRANEAN FLOWER, WAS PERILOUS, EVEN ON THE TOTALLY HORIZONTAL SURFACES IN SKIING. SO SHE STAYED HOME AND BAKED HOMEMADE BREAD. WHEN WE CAME HOME FROM A DAY OF SKIING IN HILLSBORO UPPER VILLAGE IN NEW HAMPSHIRE, OUR ANTIQUE FARM HOUSE (BUILT BETWEEN 1805 AND 1810) WAS FILLED WITH THE GLORIOUS AROMA OF FRESHLY BAKED BREAD. THE SOAP STONE STOVE IN THE BIG FARM KITCHEN RADIATED WELCOME WARMTH AND A FIRE CRACKLED IN THE OLD STONE FIREPLACE IN THE LIVING ROOM. AFTER A DAY ON THE MOUNTAIN, MOM WAS HAPPY TO SEE US, AND THE FEELING WAS VERY MUTUAL. THEN DINNER SOON FOLLOWED, FASHIONED BY OUR CUISINIERE."

Dr. Richard's comments: "Summer, 1972. Dear Stella, Andrew, family friend Dr. Macdonald Dick, and Alex, at our summer cottage on a lake called "Island Pond" in Washington, New Hampshire. We own one of the seven islands on the lake that we named "Helen's Island" in her honor and memory. 1972 was an unforgettable year for us. The Stella that you see in the photograph, young, beautiful, and happy, had been through a lot." Stella had been diagnosed with breast cancer in 1971. Surgery, chemotherapy, and radiation followed. I can imagine that she faced this challenge as she had faced other circumstances throughout her life, with strength and courage. Fortunately for Stella, her husband, and her three young children, she was completely cured. She lived to see her children grow to adulthood, and to continue her life-work as a pediatric cardiologist of the first order, loved and respected throughout the world.

CHAPTER SIX

Drs. Stella and Richard Van Praagh "An Affair of the Heart"

DRS. STELLA AND RICHARD VAN PRAAGH, CIRCA 1999

$\mathcal{D}$r. Stella Zacharioudakis and Dr. Richard Van Praagh met following a lecture he conducted on a new anatomic and developmental approach to the diagnostic understanding of congenital heart disease. Recalling their first meeting, he said, "After my presentation, a charming young lady with enormous brown eyes came up to me and started asking intelligent questions. That was Stella. We got engaged over right-heartedness and married over single ventricle."[8] The couple married in 1962, beginning a lifetime *affaire de Coeur* and professional collaboration. By 1965 the Drs. Van Praagh had three children, Andrew, Helen, and Alexander. At the time of Stella's passing in June, 2006, there were soon-to-be six grandchildren.

THIS PICTURE WAS TAKEN JUNE 20, 2001 IN THE GRAND BALLROOM OF THE BOSTON MARRIOTT LONGWARF HOTEL, AT THE FIRST RETIREMENT OF RSVP (RICHARD AND STELLA). THIS IS THE LAST PHOTOGRAPH OF THE VAN PRAAGHS AS A NUCLEAR FAMILY. PICTURED

(*L TO R*), ALEXANDER, DR. RICHARD, STELLA, HELEN, AND ANDREW. WITH THE PHOTOGRAPH, DR. RICHARD COMMENTED, "OUR DEAR DAUGHTER HELEN DIED OF MALIGNANT MELANOMA ON 9-2-01, NINE DAYS BEFORE THE TERRORISTS' ATTACK ON THE TWIN TOWERS AND THE PENTAGON. DEAR HELEN WAS VERY BRAVE. STELLA NEVER RECOVERED FROM THIS LOSS. (NOR DID ANY OF US, REALLY.)"

Dr. Richard's comments and observations concerning his life with Dr. Stella are both inspiring and poignant, and will be quoted later in this chapter. They were a "team" in the truest sense of the word, and each other's most loyal supporter. Researching, consulting, examining, sharing, teaching, and writing "in concert" with each other was their *modus operandi*. What an amazing pair! Investigative cardiologists and pathologists who founded and built the Cardiac Registry at Children's Hospital, Boston, they also received academic appointments as instructors, associates, and assistant professors at Harvard Medical School, Boston, Massachusetts. Dr. Richard Van Praagh became a Harvard professor in 1974.

Awards, honors, and recognition of their monumental contributions to medical science in the fields of pediatric cardiology and "all things relating to the heart" were frequent and deserved as the years passed.

In 1999, Dr. Stella Van Praagh was co-recipient with her husband, Dr. Richard Van Praagh, of the Distinguished Achievement Award for 1999 of the Society for Cardiovascular Pathology.

In 2001, The Cardiac Registry of Children's Hospital, Boston was named the Drs. Stella and Richard Van Praagh Cardiac Registry.

Also in 2001, The Cardiovascular Program, Children's Hospital, Boston and The National Center for Advanced Medical Education named Drs. Stella and Richard Van Praagh as the honorees for *The Third Course*, <u>Frontiers in Diagnosis</u>

and Management of Congenital Heart Disease, October 25-27, Newport, Rhode Island.

In 2004, Dr. Stella Van Praagh was co-recipient with Dr. Richard Van Praagh of the Paul Dudley White Award for 2004 of the American Heart Association.

Also in 2004, Drs. Stella and Richard Van Praagh were recognized as the honorees on Sylvia P. Griffiths Teaching Day, Division of Pediatric Cardiology, Morgan Stanley Children's Hospital of New York-Presbyterian.

After Dr. Stella's passing in 2006, the World Society for Pediatric and Congenital Heart Surgery established a lectureship in her memory. In 2007, The First Stella Van Praagh Memorial Lecture, entitled The History and Anatomy of Tetralogy of Fallot, was presented by Richard Van Praagh, MD.

In a correspondence I received from Dr. Van Praagh dated December 21, 2013, he gave an explanation of this significant honor: "The establishment of a Stella Van Praagh Memorial Lectureship is the highest honor that the pediatric and congenital heart surgeons of the world have ever bestowed on a pediatric cardiologist. A Stella Van Praagh Memorial Lecture will be given at every (biennial) meeting of the World Society, in perpetuity, for as long as the World Society exists, and no matter where the meeting occurs. Since my inaugural lecture in Washington, D.C., Stella memorial lectures have been given in Australia and in Turkey."

As I re-read those early Letters from Stella from the 1940s and 1950s, I became convinced that her memorable story deserved to be told. Her entire life reflected the enduring spirit that refuses to succumb to adversity, one which overcomes whatever circumstances occur with never-wavering purpose and tenacity. In mid-December 2013 I wrote to Dr. Richard about my plan:

> *December 13, 2013*
>
> *Dear Dr. Van Praagh:*
>
> *I am in the process of writing a story about my friend Stella entitled <u>Letters from Stella</u>. Over the years since 1946 I had saved a number of the letters that I received from her, and I think our friendship was so remarkable that it is one worth sharing.*
>
> *Although we lost touch during the intervening years from the late 1950s until the early 2000s, I would like to include a bit of biographical information about her during the years of your marriage and your cooperative medical achievements throughout the world. Of course, you have written briefly to me after her passing, and I appreciate so much knowing something of her life since I knew her. I am still so very sad that it was not possible to see her again personally after so many years had elapsed. Of course, I would appreciate your approval of my anticipated project before I move forward. Please know that you will see the completed manuscript for your critique and approval before publication, should that possibility occur.*
>
> *Sincerely,*
> *Betty Oglesbee*

What a pleasure it was to receive Dr. Richard's approval of my plan to write about Stella! A month or so later, he sent a large packet of information which thoughtfully, and helpfully, fulfilled my request.

January 29, 2014

Dear Mrs. Oglesbee,

I was amazed and dismayed to discover, just now, that a letter I had written to you on December 21st had never gotten mailed (enclosed). My apologies!

I have been very busy with medical meetings (in New York City on December 15, and in Dana Point, California, early in January). I had to give multiple presentations at both meetings.

So now, I'm looking for photos, etc., for you! I'm hoping you will not find that what I send to you is information "overload."

With every good wish,
Richard Van Praagh, MD

Dr. Van Praagh's letter of December 21, 2013, mentioned in his letter dated January 29, 2014, included the following remarks:

"Letters from Stella. What an interesting idea.
1) I approve your anticipated project.
2) Thank you for telling me that I will see the completed manuscript for my critique and approval prior to publication.
3) I shall now begin to collect photographs and information that I hope will be of interest and assistance to you.
4) All I should say at this point is that this is an amazing story."

Dr. Richard's account of their life together for forty-five productive, happy, rewarding years says it best. His presentation at the First Stella Van Praagh Memorial Lecture held in Washington, D.C. in 2007 is so inspiring, so personal, and so "from the heart" that it became an imperative part of the "Stella Story," and is reprinted here with permission.

"It is a great honor for me to give the first Stella Van Praagh Memorial Lecture, focusing no only on her, but also on the history and anatomy of tetralogy of Fallot. As most of you know, Dr. Stella was my wife and soul mate, who died of a stroke in 2006.

"Born in Rethymnon on the north shore of Crete in 1927, Stella was the third child in a family of five children. She and her family fortunately survived World War II. Stella was an eyewitness to the first airborne invasion of all time, watching from the basement of their family home as the German paratroopers descended on multicolored parachutes into their vineyard. As the dark of night descended, her father Constantine quietly told his family that they were leaving. Carrying whatever they could, they walked through terraced fields, high with un-harvested grain, up into the mountains, to their ancestral village, where they were greeted with open arms.

"Growing up, Stella was a star student, essentially always the first in her class. In 1952, she graduated from the School of Medicine of the University of Athens, Greece. Following an externship at the Children's Hospital of Athens (1953-1954), she decided to emigrate to the United States, all by herself, knowing little English....For Greek students of her time, French was the foreign language most studied.

"Following a rotating internship in Christ Hospital, Jersey City, NJ (1954-1955), she became a fellow in Pediatric Cardiology in Buffalo Children's Hospital, Buffalo, NY, with the outstanding Dr. Edward C. Lambert, followed by a residency in Pediatrics (1955-1957). Stella then became a fellow in Pediatric Cardiology at Johns Hopkins in Baltimore,

MD with Dr. Helen B. Taussig, the 'mother' of Pediatric Cardiology (1957-1958). Later (1960-1961), Stella served as a Senior Research Fellow in Pediatric Cardiology at the Hospital for Sick Children in Toronto, Canada with Dr. John D. Keith, who is widely regarded as the 'father' of Canadian pediatric cardiology.

"In 1961, Dr. Edward Lambert and Dr. Peter Vlad invited Dr. Stella Zacharioudakis to become a member of the permanent staff of the Department of Pediatric Cardiology of Buffalo Children's Hospital, an invitation which Stella happily accepted.

"Stella and I were married in 1962. Early in that year, when I told Dr. Lambert that Stella and I were engaged, he looked at me with a big smile and said, 'Richard, congratulations! You snake! You snake!' Because I was working in Toronto as a fellow in pediatric cardiology, my announcement of our engagement meant that I would be depriving Dr. Lambert and the Buffalo Children's Hospital of their new cardiologist. Big Ed, as Dr. Lambert was fondly known, knew how good Stella was.

"In 1965, Stella and I were invited by Dr. Alexander S. Nadas, Dr. Sidney Farber, and Dr. Robert F. Gross to join the staff of Children's Hospital in Boston, where we have worked ever since. We had three children in three years— Andrew (1963), Helen (1964), and Alexander (1965). I thought this was a good beginning, but Stella said to me, 'Dickie, Dickie, that's the end.' And so I learned the meaning of the old saying, 'Man proposes, but woman disposes.'

"A superb cardiologist, Dr. Stella was adored by her patients, both American and Greek. At Children's Hospital Boston, Dr. Stella was our 'Greek connection.' Patients and their parents coming from Greece were astonished to find that their Boston cardiologist knew not only what they were saying, but what they were thinking. A master teacher of congenital cardiac pathology and embryology, with emphasis on its diagnostic and surgical relevance, Stella's lectures for tired Cardiology fellows and Cardiac Surgical residents were legendary. She would often begin by serving her homemade Greek Easter bread. A superb cuisiniere, Stella made six different kinds of bread, never with a recipe. Her lectures were models of clarity and practicality. A cardiac surgical resident from South America spoke for many of our trainees when he said, 'Dr. Stella, your explanation was so clear, I thought you were speaking Spanish.'

"Dr. Stella was a linguist, a philosopher, and a philanthropist. Fluent in modern Greek, Byzantine Greek, and conversant with ancient Greek—the language of Aristotle, Plato, Aeschylus, Euripides, et al—Stella led an Ancient Greek studies group in Wellesley, MA, fondly known as the Mythology Club. They used the Loeb Classical Library bilingual editions, with English on one side and ancient Greek on the other. This way, Stella could check the accuracy of the English translation, and when necessary, improve on it. The participants, all grandmothers, not only read these books or plays, they *acted* them. And then they would discuss them—including the relevant ancient history.

"Stella gave approximately $100,000 to the renovation campaign of Harvard Medical School's Countway Library. These were her retirement savings and this magnificent library was her favorite charity.

"Dr. Stella was a 'mother' for all of our cardiology fellows and cardiac surgical residents. Stella's human qualities were as important as her professional attainments. Stella was proof that a young woman cardiologist or cardiac surgeon could be a complete, well-rounded human being: an excellent clinician, a first-class research person, a great teacher, and also a wonderful mother, wife, and amazing cuisiniere. As Stella once said to me, 'Dickie, you and I have proved that a husband and wife really can work together.'"[9]

DR. STELLA VAN PRAAGH IN HER ROLE AS CLINICIAN IN
PEDIATRIC CARDIOLOGY AT CHILDREN'S HOSPITAL BOSTON.

DR. STELLA GIVING HER FAREWELL ADDRESS
AT OUR RETIREMENT PARTY IN 2002.

AT BLUEBERRY, OUR SUMMER COTTAGE NEAR WASHINGTON, NEW HAMPSHIRE, WITH SOME OF OUR FELLOWS WHOM STELLA FONDLY CALLED OUR CARDIAC REGISTRY FAMILY. DINNER HAD JUST ENDED WITH BLUEBERRY PIE. TO STELLA'S RIGHT IS JULIA DE VIVIE, PEDIATRIC CARDIOLOGIST, HAMBURG, GERMANY.

ON STELLA'S LEFT IS CHRISTIAN KREUTZER, PEDIATRIC CARDIAC SURGEON, BUENOS AIRES, ARGENTINA. IN THE BACKGROUND IS MARIA CONCEPCION, PEDIATRIC CARDIOLOGIST IN MEXICO.

DR. STELLA AS HOSTESS, ENTERTAINING AT HOME IN
WELLESLEY, MASSACHUSETTS. CONVERSATION WITH
STELLA WAS BOTH FUN AND FASCINATING—OFTEN A REAL
EDUCATION. THIS WAS HOW THE MYTHOLOGY CLUB BEGAN—
AT THE INSISTENCE OF HER DEVOTED FRIENDS. "YOU MUST
TEACH US. WE WANT TO LEARN," THEY KEPT SAYING.

STELLA IN HER ROLE AS LOVING MOTHER AND GRANDMOTHER. THIS
PHOTO WAS TAKEN IN THE BACK GARDEN OF HELEN, OUR DEAR
DAUGHTER WHO DIED OF MALIGNANT MELANOMA IN 2001 AT THE
AGE OF 37 YEARS. HELEN IS SURVIVED BY HER HUSBAND JEAN-
PIERRE PARNAS, AND BY HER TWO SONS BENJAMIN AND DAVID.
THUS, STELLA WAS NO STRANGER TO SORROW. BUT SHE CARRIED ON
AS BRAVELY AS POSSIBLE AND TOOK JOY IN HER SONS, SON-IN-LAW,
DAUGHTERS-IN-LAW, AND GRANDCHILDREN (NOW SEVEN IN NUMBER).

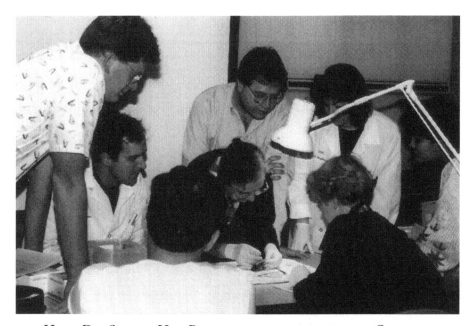

Here Dr. Stella Van Praagh is teaching in the Cardiac Registry by demonstrating and discussing congenitally malformed heart specimens. The participants included pediatric cardiology fellows, cardiac surgery residents, radiology residents, pathology residents, echocardiography technicians, operating room nurses, and visitors from other institutions. To Dr. Stella's right is Dr. Juan Campbell from Caracas, Venezuela, who is now practicing pediatric cardiology in Chicago.

Dr. Richard Van Praagh's comments relating to the image above: "Learning based on heart specimens, with a very knowledgeable guide such as Dr. Stella, is vastly superior to trying to learn from books, journals, or slide presentations. Heart specimens are 'real,' palpable, and 3-dimensional. These features are very important, particularly for interventional cardiologists and cardiac surgeons."

⁓

"Dr. Stella Van Praagh was one of the most outstanding pediatric cardiologists and perhaps pediatric cardiology pathologists of the 20th and 21st centuries, and the author or more than 110 scientific publications.

"Her understanding of ancient Greek helped make it possible to understand what Aristotle, the discoverer of the cardiovascular system, had meant by saying that normally, the human heart has three ventricles. By retranslating Aristotle's text from ancient Greek, Dr. Stella played an important role in deciphering this mystery that had gone unsolved for more than 2,300 years.

"As her achievements and honors indicate, Dr. Stella Van Praagh was a pre-eminent pediatric cardiologist and pediatric cardiac pathologist. The breadth and depth of her expertise in these two different but closely interrelated fields were unmatched. Being the soul of modesty and self-effacement, she would strongly disagree with this assessment. But for many of those who knew her, Dr. Stella Van Praagh was quite simply, incomparable."[9]

Dr. Richard Van Praagh's lecture continued with a scholarly, scientific presentation on <u>The History and Anatomy of Tetralogy of Fallot</u>. (Briefly, Dr. Arthur Fallot of Marseille, Professor of Hygiene and Legal Medicine, had coined the term *tetralogy* in his 1888 serialized reports in *Marseille Medical* in regard to four anomalies of the heart that occur together and characterize the malformation.)

In 2007, Dr. Ornella Milanesi and Dr. Bruno Marino (two of Italy's most distinguished pediatric cardiologists) on behalf of the Italian Federation of Cardiology, penned a heartwarming tribute to Dr. Stella Van Praagh with the following words:

"The Italian community of pediatric cardiologists and cardiac surgeons owes so much to Dr. Stella Van Praagh, without whom our discipline would not be at the same level in our Country.

"Since the latest 1970s and early 1980s, many of us have been trained at the Children's Hospital in Boston or had the opportunity to spend a more or less long period of time at the Cardiac Registry. Stella was, for everybody, a teacher, a mentor, a friend and a mother, teaching not only cardiac pathology and pediatric cardiology, but also the wisdom, compassion, humanity and humility with which a doctor must take care of his patients. Endowed with exceptional inner strength and fearless integrity, she always had the courage to call everything as she saw it, no matter the consequence and, also in this respect, she was a spotless model for all of us. But she was also a caring friend. Every time an Italian visitor arrived at the Cardiac Registry, Stella's first worry was to wash some interesting specimens in fresh water to demonstrate, or to ask the guest, which malformed heart among the collections he would have been interested in looking at. And her homemade bread, which she offered to all of those present--residents, visitors and pupils--was the unforgettable conclusion to every meeting.

"Sharing the same Mediterranean origins, we always felt at home at the Cardiac Registry when listening to her lessons dealing with so many different topics: cardiac pathology, pediatric cardiology, history and philosophy.

"Stella's demise has been a tremendous loss for all of us, but we will honor her memory by passing to the new generations the invaluable lessons she gave to us with her words and her life."[10]

Stella's memorial service was held at Wellesley Hills
Congregational Church in Wellesley, Massachusetts. "Many
friends and colleagues sensed that there was something
very different about Dr. Stella. Some saw her as a visionary.
Others were awed by her great inner strength and her fearless
integrity. She was also modest, self-effacing, and always anxious to help others. Dr. Stella Van Praagh was the embodi-
ment of what Socrates and Plato called virtue. She had the
courage and integrity always to call it as she saw it, no matter
how difficult or unpopular that might be. She wore many
hats, all of them well: cardiologist, pathologist, philosopher,
wife, mother, grandmother, incomparable friend, and wise
counselor."[11]

CHAPTER SEVEN

Stella Van Praagh M.D.
A Chronology

Education:
1952: University of Athens, School of Medicine, Athens, Greece

Internship and Residences:
1953-54: External Assistant, Children's Hospital of Athens University, Greece
1954-55: Rotating Intern, Christ Hospital, Jersey City, New Jersey
1955-56: Fellow in Pediatric Cardiology, Buffalo Children's Hospital, Buffalo, New York
1956-57: Resident in Pediatrics, Buffalo Children's Hospital, Buffalo, New York
1957-58: Fellow in Pediatric Cardiology and Resident Physician of the Happy Hills Convalescent Home for Children of Johns Hopkins Hospital, Baltimore, Maryland

Research Fellowships:
1960-61: Senior Research Fellow in Pediatric Cardiology, The Hospital for Sick Children, Toronto, Ontario, Canada
1961-62: Research Associate in Cardiology, Buffalo Children's Hospital, Buffalo, New York
1961-62: Instructor in Pediatrics, University of Buffalo Medical School, Buffalo, New York
1962-63: Senior Research Fellow in Pediatric Cardiology, The Hospital for Sick Children, Toronto, Ontario, Canada

Academic Appointments:
1959-60: Cardiologist-in-Charge, Children's Hospital of Athens University, Athens, Greece
1964-65: Associate in Pediatrics, Harvard Medical School, Boston, Massachusetts
1965-71: Instructor in Pediatrics, Harvard Medical School, Boston, Massachusetts
1971-92: Assistant Professor in Pathology, Harvard Medical School, Boston, Massachusetts
1992- : Assistant Professor in Pathology, Harvard Medical School, Boston, Massachusetts (*Emerita*)

Hospital Appointments:
1964-65: Assistant Cardiologist, The Children's Memorial Hospital, Chicago, Illinois
1965-92: Associate in Cardiology, Children's Hospital, Boston, Massachusetts
1992- : Associate in Cardiology, Children's Hospital, Boston, Massachusetts (*Emerita*)

Richard Van Praagh, M.D.
A Chronology

Education:
1954: M.D., Faculty of Medicine, University of Toronto

Internship and Residencies:
1954-55: Rotating Intern, Toronto General Hospital, Toronto
1955-56: Intern in Pediatrics, Hospital for Sick Children, Toronto
1956-57: Assistant Resident in Pathology, Children's Hospital Medical Center, Boston
1957-58: Senior Resident in Pediatrics, Children's Hospital Medical Center, Boston
1958-59: Senior Resident in Internal Medicine, Sunnybrook Hospital, Toronto

Research Fellowships:
1959-60: Fellow in Pediatric Cardiology, Johns Hopkins Hospital, Baltimore
1960-61: Fellow in Cardiopulmonary Physiology, Mayo Clinic, Rochester, Minnesota
1961-63: Senior Research Fellow in Pediatric Cardiology, Hospital for Sick Children, Toronto

Academic Appointments:
1964-65: Instructor in Pediatrics, Northwestern University Medical School, Chicago
1965-65: Assistant Professor of Pediatrics, Northwestern University Medical School, Chicago

1965-67: Clinical Associate in Pathology, Harvard Medical School, Boston
1967-70: Assistant Clinical Professor of Pathology, Harvard Medical School, Boston
1970-73: Associate Professor of Pathology, Harvard Medical School, Boston
1974-2001: Professor of Pathology, Harvard Medical School, Boston
2001- : Professor of Pathology, *(Emeritus)*, Harvard Medical School, Boston

Hospital Appointments:
1965: Director of Cardiac Pathology and Embryology, Research Associate in Cardiology, and Research Associate Cardiac Surgery, Children's Hospital Medical Center, Boston
1974- : Research Associate in Cardiac Surgery, Children's Hospital Medical Center, Boston

Other Professional Positions and Visiting Appointments:
1963-64: Associate Pathologist, Congenital Heart Disease Research and Training Center, Hektoen Institute for Medical Research, Chicago
1964-65: Assistant Director, Congenital Heart Disease Research and Training Center, Hektoen Institute for Medical Research, Chicago
1966-66: Visiting Scientist, Department of Embryology, Carnegie Institution of Washington, Baltimore

CHAPTER EIGHT

My "Stellar" Friend
Stella Zacharioudak is
Van Praagh M.D.

$\mathcal{S}$ometimes significant events in life "just happen." There are times when we are enriched and blessed through unexpected, inexplicable coincidences that "just happen."

Who could have ever anticipated that two young girls from totally different worlds, living oceans apart, could become friends as the result of a tiny handmade bag filled with soap and toothpaste? It "just happened."

Looking back, I wish that Stella and I had not "lost touch" over those many intervening years. Perhaps that, too, "just happened."

It has been a privilege for me to honor Stella in this small way, in the telling of her story as revealed in the "Letters from Stella" from the 1940s and 1950s, as well as those I received from her in 2005. From the very beginning, her unswerving commitment to achieving her dreams never lessened. Her "life well lived" reflects the best qualities of the human spirit. She loved with all her heart, she cared deeply for the health and well-being of those in need, and she unselfishly gave of herself for the betterment of others. All her inspiring attributes, as described throughout the pages of this book, were the reason she was such a beloved, brilliant doctor. I am so very, very proud to have known her!

Dr. Stella Zacharioudakis Van Praagh truly made a difference in this world, and that didn't "just happen."

ENDNOTES

1. 1995 interview with Tony Ball, Supply Sergeant for POW Camp San Augustine, 1944-1946.
2. Proctor, Ben H., *World War II, Handbook of Texas* online. http://www.tshaonline.org/handbook
3. *ACE of Greece.* http://aceofgreece.wordpress.com
4. *World War II: Battle of Crete,* http://militaryhistory.about.com
5. *Military History of Greece during World War II.* http://en.wikipedia.org
6. Bellis, Mary, *The History of Nylon Stockings.* http://inventors.about.com
7. *Texas City Disaster.* http://en.wikipedia.org
8. Marquand, Bryan, Interview with Dr. Richard Van Praagh, Boston Globe, June 9, 2006
9. Van Praagh, R: *The First Stella Van Praagh Memorial Lecture: The History and Anatomy of Tetralogy of Fallot.* Semin Thorac Cardiovase Surg Pediatr Card Surg Ann 2009; 12:19-38.
10. (Dr.) Milanesi, Ornella and (Dr.) Marino, Bruno, *Stella Van Praagh* (obituary), Italian Federation of Cardiology. http://journals.lww.com/jcardiovascularmedicine/Citation/2007/01000
11. Obituary, *Stella Van Praagh MD: World Famous Pediatric Cardiologist, Pathologist, and Philosopher,* June 2006.

Made in the USA
San Bernardino, CA
02 June 2018